Original title:
Peachy Keen Moments

Copyright © 2025 Creative Arts Management OÜ
All rights reserved.

Author: Ethan Prescott
ISBN HARDBACK: 978-1-80586-454-7
ISBN PAPERBACK: 978-1-80586-926-9

Outputs of Endless Gratitude

In a world where clumsiness reigns,
I tripped on my shoelace, but it made me gain.
A giggle from strangers, a shared little glance,
I danced like a fool—oh, what a chance!

Morning coffee spilled, a splash in my shoes,
My cat did a leap, took the shirts as his muse.
Laughter erupted, what chaos it bore,
Thankful for mishaps, who could ask for more?

Friends gathered 'round, a potluck delight,
Burnt casserole aroma that took flight.
We toasted to choices, both silly and grand,
With grateful hearts, we made our own brand.

In absurdity's glow, we find our true spark,
From scrapes and from laughs, we light up the dark.
So here's to the blunders, the quirks of this race,
In each little moment, we find our own grace.

Sugar-Dusted Smiles

A sprinkle of laughter, oh so bright,
With sticky fingers, we take a bite.
Syrupy giggles, they fill the air,
Silly faces without a care.

Sweet surprises in every nook,
We read the day like a comic book.
With joy, we dance in a sugar haze,
In a world that spins with silly ways.

Moments like Ripe Fruit

Snapshot memories, juicy and bold,
Fruity laughter, never grows old.
Each tick of time is a tasty tease,
Bursting flavors carried on the breeze.

Sunshine ripens our playful hearts,
In this orchard, fun never departs.
Silly antics, each one a gem,
Life's a picnic, let's say 'Amen'!

The Sweetness of Time Unraveled

Tickle my time, make it sway,
With honeyed giggles along the way.
Moments unravel like candy threads,
Wrapping up laughter in cozy beds.

Tick-tock, we play in twisted fun,
A carousel ride when the day is done.
Sweet memories blend into a swirl,
With every chuckle, life starts to twirl.

Laughter Beneath the Blossoms

Under petals, we spin and glide,
Where humor blooms like a joyful tide.
With a wink and a chuckle, we dance in glee,
Finding punchlines on every tree.

In the garden of giggles, we play peek-a-boo,
With blossoms giggling, their colors so true.
Nature's humor spills into the scene,
Where laughter reigns and we stay serene.

The Magic of Here and Now

A splash of juice, a silly grin,
Chasing shadows where giggles begin.
The sun shines bright, it's hard to frown,
In the loudest joys, we wear our crown.

Wobbly bikes and ice cream cones,
Bouncing laughter in playful tones.
Lost in games, we're never late,
Every moment feels like fate.

Little Wonders in Bloom

A tiny bug with polka dots,
Waves hello in the sun's hot spots.
Missed the train? Just dance and sing,
With each small glitch, let joy take wing.

Bubbles float on a gentle breeze,
Tickling noses, drawing squeals with ease.
Nature laughs in rustling leaves,
Each twist and turn, the heart receives.

Fables of Joyful Discovery

A cat in socks that slips down stairs,
Chasing tails with wild flares.
Jumper cables for a toy car,
Adventures wander, near and far.

Rainy days and puddle pools,
Make-believe in backyard schools.
Fortresses made of couch and sheet,
Imagined worlds are oh-so-sweet.

Symphony of Blossoms

Dancing petals, a lively show,
Flowers wave as breezes flow.
A slight surprise, a candy bee,
Chasing joy, wild and free.

Echoes of laughter fill the air,
Muffin crumbs and splatters everywhere.
Pet rocks sing in a silly tune,
Under the watch of a laughing moon.

Breezes that Carry Delight

Winds weave laughter through the trees,
A squirrel dances, doing as he please.
With picnic spreads and soda pops,
Our cheerful giggles never stop.

Kites flutter high, a vibrant show,
Chasing shadows where daisies grow.
Sunshine bounces off our bright hats,
We tumble down with playful splats.

Sun-Kissed Memories

Golden rays dance on our cheek,
Like playful tickles, strong yet weak.
We chase the warmth with joyful screams,
In a world that sparkles with silly dreams.

Ice cream smudged on our eager faces,
Laughter echoes in open spaces.
Butterflies flutter, oh so spry,
While we attempt a graceful fly.

Candied Dreams and Garden Scenes

Bees buzz sweetly around the blooms,
We giggle as a flower looms.
Cupcakes tempting with their charm,
We steal a bite, not a single alarm.

Sunflowers reaching for the sky,
We stumble near, oh my, oh my!
With nature's giggles at our side,
Adventure calls, we cannot hide.

The Taste of Warm Embrace

Hot cocoa spills, a marshmallow fight,
Laughter lingers in the warm night.
With goofy hats and silly wigs,
We cha-cha dance like goofy pigs.

Cozy chatters by the fire's glow,
We share our tales, our secrets flow.
A fruit-flavored toast to all we claim,
In this moment, we're all the same.

Delicate Laughter Beneath Trees

Under branches, kids play fair,
Giggles soar through the warm air.
Silly faces, wild and free,
Sneaky squirrels dance in glee.

A frisbee flies, a yelp, a catch,
Everyone's caught in a great mismatch.
A pie made fresh, it flips and flops,
Laughter erupts as it splats and drops.

Sunkissed Smiles and Memories

Sunshine glows on faces wide,
Mom's new hat, a playful ride.
Sandals slip, and laughter spills,
Each moment sweet, like candy thrills.

A dog runs by with such a flair,
Chasing shadows, without a care.
Sticky fingers, ice cream drips,
Falling laughter, joyful flips.

Honeyed Days of Delight

Beehive buzz and scents so sweet,
Kids run fast on little feet.
Picnic spread, a feast of fun,
Who dropped this cake? Oh, everyone!

Chasing dreams by the riverside,
"Catch me if you can," is the pride.
A splash here, a giggle there,
Days like these, nothing can compare.

Warmth Beneath a Peach Sky

Clouds like cotton, floating high,
Silly hats tipped slightly awry.
Bubbles dance on winds so light,
Even bugs seem to frolic bright.

A jumble of friends in a big heap,
Squeals of joy, no time for sleep.
Chasing sunsets with painted grins,
In this laughter, joy begins.

Embracing Life's Juiciness

Biting into laughter, juicy and bright,
Every messy moment feels just right.
Slipping on smiles, we dance in a swirl,
Life's a fruit salad, let's give it a twirl.

Juggling our worries, we toss them away,
Chasing the sunshine, come out and play.
Dripping with joy, we're splashed with good cheer,
In this sweet chaos, we have nothing to fear.

Kaleidoscope of Colorful Moments

Swirling through laughter, a whirlwind of glee,
Every vibrant chuckle is wild and free.
Colors of giggles light up the day,
Painting our worries in hues that just play.

Tickling the fancy of fun, oh so bright,
Spinning through life like a kite in the light.
Every twist and turn brings a grin on our face,
In this mosaic of joy, we find our own space.

Starlit Secrets

Whispers and chuckles beneath the night sky,
Shooting stars giggle as they wink and fly.
Ticklish secrets shared with the moon,
Dancing in shadows, we swoon to the tune.

Cosmic confessions, a celestial jest,
Finding the joy in a starlit quest.
Laughter like comets, they light up the scene,
Under these twinkling gems, we float in between.

Underneath the Fragrant Canopy

Nestled in blossoms, we cradle delight,
Scented stories tickle our senses tonight.
Petals of laughter fall soft as a breeze,
Life's a wild garden, let's plant a tease.

Beneath the green hugs of nature's surprise,
We giggle like children with wide-open eyes.
Each rustle and whisper, a joke from the leaves,
In this fragrant embrace, our heart gladly weaves.

Sweet Nothings in the Breeze

A squirrel stole my sandwich,
As I sat on the grass.
I laughed so hard I tipped over,
And now I need a new class.

The wind whispered secrets,
That only I could decode.
My hat flew off to join it,
In a madcap, playful road.

Clouds danced like jellybeans,
In the sky, so spry and bright.
I tried to catch one swiftly,
But it gave me quite a fright.

With friends all laughing near me,
We shared a moment's glee.
The world was full of nonsense,
And I just wanted to be free.

Dreamy Escapades of Youth

We built a fort from cushions,
And claimed it as our throne.
With stickers on the windows,
We ruled the world alone.

A dragon made from laundry,
Guarded treasures, so we thought.
But it turned out to be mum's robe,
And more laundry was forgot.

We raced our bikes to nowhere,
Donuts made our tires squeal.
But the ice cream truck was calling,
And we couldn't miss that meal.

Under the stars, we giggled,
And made wishes on our dreams.
Youth is ever fleeting,
Like life's most vibrant schemes.

Whimsical Journeys Through Time

I found a door to nowhere,
A portal made of dreams.
It led me to a teacup,
Where time stopped, or so it seems.

We sipped on rainbow juices,
With elves and jealous frogs.
They danced upon the table,
While we laughed and ate hot dogs.

The clock spun like a ballerina,
Chasing kittens and goldfish too.
We hopped from year to year,
In a rush to feel the new.

But soon enough it told us,
That all good things must close.
So we said farewell to magic,
With a wink and secret prose.

Tasting Life, One Moment at a Time

I bit into a donut,
And sprinkles flew like stars.
Old ladies at the bakery,
They gawked and gave me scars.

Chocolate dripped from fingers,
As I savored every bite.
There's laughter in the chaos,
And crumbs that feel just right.

With a cherry on the top,
I took a giant scoop.
The flavors burst like fireworks,
In my happy little loop.

Moments like sweet candy,
So sugary and divine.
Each one a little treasure,
In this life of yours and mine.

Hues of Happiness

In a world of bright balloons,
We danced beneath the moon.
Ice cream dripped on tiny hands,
Laughter echoed through the lands.

With silly hats and goofy grins,
We spun around, the fun begins.
Colors splashed, like paint on walls,
We painted joy, and missed our falls.

A rubber chicken in my pack,
Tickles and giggles, no way to lack.
With every step, we stomped and pranced,
In a whirl of joy, we took our chance.

Sunshine bursts in every frame,
We're the stars in this wild game.
Through slips and trips, our spirits soar,
In hues of happiness, forever more.

Golden Hours by the River

Mismatched socks, a charming sight,
We soaked in sun, from morn 'til night.
Skipping rocks with all our might,
Who knew splashes could bring such delight?

The river sang a silly tune,
We danced like ducks under the moon.
With sandwiches stuck to our face,
Laughter flowed, outpaced the race.

A frog jumped in, a splash so wide,
We all took cover, giggling with pride.
Canoes flipped over, oh what a mess,
But smiles and snacks were pure happiness!

As sun went down, we'd tell our tales,
With jokes and jests like skipping rails.
In golden hours, let's not grow old,
With fun and laughter, life unfolds.

Juicy Secrets Shared

Under the shade of a sun-soaked tree,
We whispered secrets, wild and free.
With fruit so ripe, we took a bite,
Sticky fingers, oh what a sight!

Giggles erupted, juice on our chins,
Telling tales of our silly sins.
Through juicy smiles, mischief was planned,
In our little club, we took a stand.

With gumball machines and pop rocks galore,
We swapped our treasures, who could want more?
The secrets flowed like lemonade,
In a summer haze, no promises made.

With each new whisper, laughter ignites,
In this silly world, everything excites.
So raise your glass and give a cheer,
To juicy secrets and friendships dear!

A Serenade of Summer Days

With hats askew and sunscreen smeared,
We danced on grass, absolutely weird.
Popcorn kernels flying high,
As we faced the sun in a joyful cry.

Slip-n-slide splashes, laughter galore,
Our wild adventures, who could ask for more?
The ice cream truck, like a sweet serenade,
With wacky flavors, we weren't afraid.

Sunset picnics, under skies so vast,
We'd tell old tales, and make them last.
With every giggle, the world spun round,
In summer days, pure joy is found.

As stars peeked in, the fun still stayed,
In this whimsical life we gladly played.
So here's to laughter, let's raise a toast,
To a summer serenade we cherish most!

Happiness on the Horizon

Sunshine spills like melted cheese,
Laughter dances in the breeze,
Chasing shadows in a race,
With a sticky smear on my face.

Clouds transform to furry sheep,
As I tumble, roll, and leap,
Jellybeans fall from the sky,
Every bounce a sweet surprise.

Giggling till my sides do ache,
Snow cones melting in the lake,
Each small moment feels so grand,
With sprinkles scattered on the sand.

Happiness flows like lemonade,
Spilled on my toes in parade,
With every sip, I lose my fears,
Chasing dreams on giggly cheers.

The Beauty of Colorful Daydreams

Cotton candy clouds float by,
Tickled giggles fill the sky,
Bouncing thoughts like rubber balls,
Echoing through candy halls.

Raindrops giggle as they land,
Wobbling jelly on the sand,
Whimsical thoughts swirl like ice,
Life's an odd yet charming dice.

Butterflies with polka dots,
Paint the world in silly spots,
Every blink a chance to play,
Chasing rainbows every day.

In my head, it's quite a ride,
With a pogo stick as my guide,
Each mishap a reason to cheer,
Did I just trip? Oh dear, oh dear!

A Daydream Painted in Light

In a world where giggles grow,
Where jellybeans dance in a row,
Sunny rays paint every scene,
Making the mundane feel like a dream.

Crayons spill from skies above,
Coloring life with endless love,
Every step a wacky twist,
In this wild adventure list.

Lemonade rivers flow with glee,
Ticklish waves inviting me,
Splashing through the golden light,
Finding joy in silly sights.

Mirthful grins and silly hats,
Chasing squirrels, avoiding spats,
In this canvas bright and free,
Every day a jubilee.

Wildflower Whispers in the Sunshine

Wildflowers giggle in the park,
Whisper secrets till it's dark,
Bumblebees buzz in delight,
In dance-offs, they are the light.

Sunshine spills like a spilled bean,
Turning everything to a scene,
Each sprout boasts a funky style,
As we prance with endless smiles.

Grass stains on my favorite jeans,
Set the stage for silly scenes,
Chasing rainbows, feeling spry,
With laughter lifting us up high.

Picnics filled with jiggly treats,
Silly voices mix with beats,
Every moment, wild and free,
In this joyful jubilee.

Bubbles of Bliss in the Orchard

In a land of sweet delight,
Bubbles float, oh what a sight!
Laughter echoes through the trees,
Joyful moments on the breeze.

Bees are buzzing, not a care,
Chasing friends without a scare.
Giggling children, running wild,
Life is grand, we're all beguiled.

Jars of jam and sticky hands,
Muffins baked from secret plans.
Silly faces, pie on nose,
Lemonade spills in joyful prose.

Under branches, shade we seek,
With ice cream cones, it's quite the peak.
Savoring sweets while time drips slow,
In this orchard, our hearts aglow.

Fleeting Moments in the Shade

Swinging high on ropes of fun,
Shadows dance as we all run.
Chasing dreams beneath the trees,
With laughter carried on the breeze.

A mischievous dog steals a shoe,
While we yell, 'That's mine, who knew?'
Fingers sticky from the treats,
Life is more than just repeats.

Pies that wobble, snacks gone fast,
Moments fleeting, but they last.
Sips of soda, silly games,
Every laugh, a spark that flames.

Shade embraces, laughter spills,
In these moments, joy fulfills.
Playing hide and seek with fate,
Forget the time, we're truly great!

Tapestry of Fleeting Joy

Threads of laughter in the air,
Growing memories, light as hair.
Each bright giggle weaves a story,
In this tapestry of glory.

Jumping puddles with a splash,
Every second a joyous dash.
Tickling toes in summer pools,
In these shades, we break the rules.

Glimmers of sunshine winking bright,
Butterflies dance, oh what a sight!
Chasing dreams like kites in flight,
Fleeting moments, pure delight.

Pies on windows, smells so sweet,
Here in laughter, life's complete.
With friends around, let spirits soar,
In our hearts, we want for more!

Soft Petals and Sunny Skies

Under the blooms, we lay and stare,
Soft petals drift through the air.
Playful winds whisper our names,
In this garden, life's a game.

Sunshine tickles, joy ignites,
Lively beyond our wildest sights.
We leap and bound, like birds in flight,
Skipping stones with sheer delight.

Chocolate smeared on cheeky grins,
Moments fly, but joy just begins.
Rolling in grass, feeling so free,
Tickled by branches from the tree.

In this realm of daisies and dreams,
Life isn't quite as hard as it seems.
Each soft laughter, a brilliant prize,
Entwined in soft petals and sunny skies.

Playful Shadows in the Light

Bouncing ball upon the grass,
Silly dogs, they leap and pass.
Chasing tails without a care,
Laughter echoes, fills the air.

Sunshine dapples on my nose,
Ticklish breeze, oh how it blows.
Squirrels dance, they jump and twist,
In this moment, joy persists.

Friends unite for silly games,
Silly hats with vibrant names.
A pie that sails, a cake that flies,
With every snack, we share our sighs.

Tickled toes in sandy shores,
Impromptu giggles, open doors.
A dance-off with a wobbly grin,
Let the playful antics begin!

Radiance in Every Bite

Chocolate sprinkles, ice cream scoops,
Laughter mingles with the troops.
Each bite bursting with delight,
Sweet surprises in every bite.

Sugar highs and silly games,
Syrupy smiles and funny names.
Floating donuts, jellybeans too,
In this feast, we're never blue.

Cake fights in the afternoon,
Whipped cream smiles, we're over the moon.
The fruit parade rolls on the floor,
Mango madness, we shout for more!

Giggling chefs with crazy hats,
Cooking up some wacky chats.
The mixer spins, but so do we,
Delicious chaos, joy runs free!

Glimmers of Bliss

Twinkling stars in the vibrant night,
Fireflies dance, a charming sight.
Whimsical whispers of friendly cheers,
Laughter bubbles, dissolving fears.

The moon wears a smile, oh so bright,
Jumpy shadows play with delight.
Each giggle echoes through the trees,
Where joy flutters on a gentle breeze.

Cupcakes sailing on clouds of cream,
Like frosting dreams, we laugh and beam.
Silly hats and playful pranks,
In a world of fun, we give our thanks.

Balancing spoons in a funny race,
Tiny feet in a playful chase.
Spinning in circles, let's not stop,
In these moments, we're on top!

Evaporating Worries

Bubbles floating in the blue,
Each one carries dreams anew.
With a pop, they drift away,
Leaving troubles where they lay.

Giggles bouncing off the walls,
Laughter echoes through the halls.
Funny faces and silly jokes,
Clearing clouds that once were blokes.

Kites that soar above our heads,
Spinning tales, no time for dreads.
Cotton candy at the fair,
Every worry disappears in air.

Jumping puddles, splashes fly,
Raindrops tickle as they cry.
With a smile, we say goodbye,
To every frown that dares to try!

Luminous Joy Underneath the Canopy

Underneath the leafy shade,
Butterflies dance, serenade.
Squirrels chatter, nuts in tow,
A picnic spread, the ants will show.

Laughter echoes through the trees,
Tickled toes in warm, soft breeze.
A sandwich thief, the raccoon steals,
What's that noise? Oh, it just squeals!

Juicy spills and giggles fly,
Chasing shadows, oh me, oh my!
A lemon pie, a slippery treat,
Who needs chairs when grass is sweet?

Wrapped in sunshine, carefree fun,
Chasing warmth till day is done.
With every laugh, a memory made,
In the glow where dreams invade.

Heartbeats in Sunlight

With every heartbeat, sunshine glows,
A frolic dance, the happiness flows.
A bubble pops, laughter ensues,
Ping pong balls, silly to lose.

Chasing shadows, we skip along,
Singing sweetly our silly song.
The ice cream melts, a sticky race,
Wipe that smudge off your face!

We twirl like tops, our joy uncontained,
Caught in giggles, completely untrained.
Watch out for splashes, the water's near,
A slip and a splash, oh my, what a cheer!

In heartbeats quick as summer flies,
We dance beneath these sunny skies.
With every laugh, the day resigns,
To memories sweet as fruit, life's wines.

Sunkissed Lullabies

A warm breeze whispers lullabies,
While lazy clouds drift through the skies.
Ice cream drips upon your hand,
Sun-kissed laughter, oh what a band!

Crickets chirp a silly tune,
The stars come out, oh so soon.
Frogs in chorus, a ribbit fest,
Nature's laughter, simply the best.

Sandcastles rise, then tumble down,
As seagulls chuckle, waddle around.
A beach ball bounces, off the wrong feet,
Rolling along, does anybody eat?

With every giggle, the night unfolds,
A treasure trove of laughter told.
In every wink, the secrets align,
Sunkissed moments, oh how they shine!

Warmth in Every Glimpse

There's warmth in every glance we share,
The silly antics beyond compare.
Naps in hammocks, snoozing like logs,
In every chuckle, we welcome the frogs.

Chasing rainbows and wild butterflies,
With every hop, the laughter flies.
On double-dares, we take the leap,
Lucky charm in the laughter deep.

Spinning like tops under gleeful skies,
The world a stage for our wild highs.
Marshmallow roasts 'til the sun says bye,
With every smile, we reach for the sky.

Reflecting warmth in every voice,
In joyous cracks, we find our choice.
These moments linger, brightly lit,
In laughter wrapped, our hearts are hit.

Melting into Laughter

In a world where giggles reign,
Silly hats and pies of grain,
We chase our shadows, duck and weave,
A dance of joy, so hard to believe.

With tickles traded in the park,
And ice cream spills when it's not dark,
We laugh till our sides ache and moan,
These moments hum, a funny tone.

A cat who leaps in wild surprise,
Chasing its tail under bright skies,
Each stumble is a comedic feat,
As we bobble, wiggle, and twirl our feet.

So here's to laughter, loud and clear,
The spice of life we hold so dear,
In every snort and chuckle grand,
These melting moments, just as planned.

Afternoons Dripping with Joy

The sun hangs low, a lazy friend,
Ice tea spills, let the giggles blend,
Sunscreen noses, watermelon bites,
We play hopscotch, in silly fights.

With bubbles floating, we jump the rope,
A game of tag fuels our hope,
Silly songs and wild charades,
Laughter dances in playful parades.

A kite gets stuck in neighbor's trees,
While antics blow like summer breeze,
Each moment adds a pinch of cheer,
A snapshot held, so crystal clear.

As shadows stretch, we lay on grass,
With shared secrets and silly sass,
These afternoons, forever cling,
In joy we sing, let laughter spring.

The Art of Simple Pleasures

A cookie jar holds tales untold,
Each crumb a memory, fun and bold,
We bake and laugh, a floury scene,
With kitchen battles, oh so keen.

Jumping puddles in rubber boots,
While dodging raindrops like little brutes,
A dance of joy with laughter's flair,
Oh, simple pleasures, beyond compare.

The art of slipping on a slide,
With giggles echoing far and wide,
Rolling down hills, grass stains galore,
Who needs a plan? Let's explore!

We share our secrets, dreams set free,
In every moment, just you and me,
These simple joys all wrapped in cheer,
The art of laughter, held so dear.

A Sprinkle of Sunshine

In a world of silly hats and puns,
We chase the clouds and dance with runs,
With lemonade smiles and winks so bright,
Each moment drips with pure delight.

The cat who snorts while chasing tails,
And friends who send the best of emails,
When laughter blooms like flowers in spring,
A sprinkle of joy is what we bring.

We play with shadows, we jump and gleam,
Creating chaos like in a dream,
With water balloons and high-flying kites,
Each splash ignites our silly delights.

So here's to the sunshine, bright and bold,
In every giggle, our laughter unfolds,
These moments sprinkled with joy so fine,
Wrap us in laughter, forever entwined.

Juicy Reflections of Joy

In the orchard where we play,
Baskets tumble, what a day!
Laughing at the fruit that falls,
Catching whispers through the halls.

With sticky fingers, we delight,
Dancing shadows, pure and bright.
Flying seeds in our grand cheer,
Oh, the memories we hold dear!

Hiccups from the juice we drink,
Giggling now, we hardly think.
Swaying branches, a clownish show,
Who knew fruit could steal the glow?

Every bite a funny tale,
Laughter ripples like a sail.
Sweet juiciness on our lips,
We're the masters of these quips!

Sunlit Serenades

Underneath the sun's embrace,
Ripe dreams dance in every place.
Silly squirrels dash and tease,
Chasing shadows in the breeze.

Jokes on branches, laughter flows,
Who knew fruits could wear such clothes?
Cherries dressed like tiny hats,
Each one gives us silly spats.

As we pluck these bright delights,
Joy erupts in vivid sights.
Sipping juice from wild balloons,
We become the jester's tunes!

Here beneath the golden beams,
Sunshine fills our goofy dreams.
In the laughter of the hour,
We're a band of fruiting power!

A Symphony of Ripeness

A symphony of giggles rise,
As plums play peek, oh what a surprise!
Bananas dance and apples sing,
In this fruity, funny swing.

With every crunch, a note we crack,
Silly echoes bounce right back.
Melons rolling, pure delight,
We'll keep singing day and night.

Jams and jests, they intertwine,
Create a feast that feels divine.
Syrupy moments, laughter bursts,
Joyful flavors quench our thirsts.

In this orchard, life is grand,
We're the jolly fruit band!
A melodious, nutty feast,
Our sweet chuckles never cease.

The Flavor of Serenity

Serenity served on a plate,
Juicy bites that make us create.
Lemon laughs, a zesty twist,
In this flavor, we can't resist.

With every nibble, giggles bloom,
Nature's sweets make spirits zoom.
Tasting joy in every hue,
On this journey, me and you.

Fruits of life like little clowns,
Tickling souls and chasing frowns.
Dancing vines with zestful cheer,
Bring us laughter, year by year.

So let us savor, let us play,
In this orchard, come what may.
Each ripe moment fills our hearts,
In fruity joy, the fun imparts!

Dancing with the Sun

We twirl in shadows, light on our toes,
Chasing sunbeams where the warm wind blows.
Flip-flops flapping, laughter fills the air,
Sun-kissed giggles, what a sight to wear.

With every step, the grass winks at me,
A butterfly whispers, 'Come, dance, be free.'
An ice cream cone leans, slightly askew,
But who needs to balance when joy tastes so true?

Slipping on caramel, oh what a spree,
As sticky fingers wave, you laugh with glee.
The sun pulls us closer, oh what a tease,
Like a warm hug, it makes our hearts freeze.

So let's spin under rays, let the music play,
In this golden moment, forever we stay.
With silly hats dancing, oh what a thrill,
Life's silly jests always fit the bill.

Fragrant Delights of the Season

In the market, blooms of every hue,
Whiff of berries, smiles anew.
A tomato trip, oh what a sight,
Rolling right past shows the day's delight.

Cherries giggle, plump on their branch,
Peaches do a shimmy, ready to prance.
Grab a bouquet, tangled with glee,
Nature's odd jokes, like a stand-up spree.

Cabbages grumble, broccoli frowns,
Yet humor abounds in these veggie towns.
Sprigs of mint laughing, fresh on the breeze,
Keep your nose ready for whimsical tease.

So we savor each moment, we munch and we munch,
In this fragrant festival, we leap with a crunch.
Nature's funny side is the art of surprise,
As laughter blooms brightly, and boredom just dies.

Time Pausing with a Sigh

Tick-tock, tick-tock, oh what a game,
Time laughs at schedules, never feels the same.
With careless giggles, it stretches and bends,
Turning minutes to laughter, where humor transcends.

We rest on a cloud, coffee mugs high,
With a sip and a snort, we bid troubles goodbye.
In moments like these, the world's better dressed,
With laughter sewn in, we've truly been blessed.

An hour slips by, yet why should we rage?
Time's best-kept secret is its comic stage.
Playing hide and seek with past and with future,
It winks at the chaos, like one cheeky tutor.

So let's pause for a breath, with crumbs on our face,
Dive headfirst in joy, what a wild race!
Time winks in delight, as we hold on tight,
To moments that sparkle in carefree delight.

Mirth Amongst the Trees

Under canopies green, we gather and cheer,
Squirrels are giggling, as if we are near.
With each rustle of leaves, a story unfolds,
Of branches that dance and leaves that are bold.

A breeze tosses hats, a tumble of fun,
While picnics get messy, oh what a run!
Bubbles float by, the sun dappled scene,
Nature's own laughter, glowing and keen.

Branches bow low, low with a laugh,
Tickling our toes, as we share in the craft.
A swing set swings, stories leap high,
With echoes of giggles that reach for the sky.

So we bask in the joy, let's play and rejoice,
In mirth amongst trees, listen to our voice.
For laughter is wild, like the roots of a tree,
In this merry dance, we're forever carefree.

Ripened Dreams Under Blue Skies

Under skies so bright and clear,
We danced with joy, let out a cheer.
A picnic spread with tasty treats,
And ants that marched with swift little feet.

The fruits were ripe, the laughter high,
We tossed the seeds and watched them fly.
One landed square on grandpa's hat,
He swatted at it, like a curious cat.

A game of tag amidst the trees,
We zigged and zagged with the breeze.
But tripped and tumbled on the ground,
And giggles echoed all around.

With juice-stained shirts and silly grins,
We made our bets on who would win.
The race to finish every snack,
But who would come in first? Whack-a-mole attack!

Echoes of Laughter Amongst Blooms

In the garden, petals swirl,
Buzzy bees and twirling girls.
We dodged and dived through flowers bright,
And wore their colors, oh what a sight!

A soft breeze tickled our noses,
As we struck silly poses.
One fell flat in a flower bed,
With daisies blooming on her head.

We chased the butterflies in flight,
And giggled at the silly sight.
A blossom landed on my shoe,
I yelled, "It's magic!" Yes, it's true!

As petals rained from skies above,
We danced around, filled with love.
But after sneezes, oh what a sound,
We laughed till we fell on the ground!

A Crisp Evening's Embrace

As daylight fades, the moon comes out,
We gather 'round, and share a shout.
The stars appear, a twinkling show,
And roasted marshmallows, oh how they glow!

The night is filled with tales so grand,
Of silly pranks that went unplanned.
One friend tried to catch a firefly,
And ended up with a splat and a pie!

The crackle of fire and tasty s'mores,
We joked and laughed till our cheeks were sore.
One took a tumble, oh what a sight,
And we rolled with laughter, pure delight!

As shadows danced, we played charades,
Acting out antics with silly parades.
The crisp night air, our joy ablaze,
A memory made in fun-filled ways!

Nature's Sweetest Confessions

With berry bushes thick and lush,
We gathered fruit in quite a rush.
A juicy bite, oh what a treat,
But watch out for the sticky feet!

The birds above joined in the fun,
Singing sweetly, a playful run.
We mimicked their songs, off-key and loud,
And laughed at our voices, so far from proud.

The sun dipped low, the sky ablaze,
As we twirled and danced through the maze.
One lost their shoe, oh what a sight,
Chasing laughter in the fading light!

With arms full of fruit and hearts so free,
We declared, "Nature's the best for me!"
In the sweetest moments, laughter flows,
In fields where joy and silliness grows.

Moments That Melt Like Summer's Warmth

The ice cream drips down my hand,
Laughter echoes all around the land.
Squirrels dance, stealing all the snacks,
We chase them off without any hacks.

A kite flies high, snagged on a tree,
While birds scold us, oh so free.
A slip on grass, then a loud cheer,
We roll like tumbleweeds, have no fear.

Sunburned noses and carefree shouts,
Mixing lemonade with playful bouts.
The grill's on fire, not from the meat,
But from dad's antics, off his feet.

As golden hour wraps us tight,
We revel in laughter, feeling bright.
These moments melt, like ice in the sun,
Together we laugh, we've already won.

The Symphony of Fruity Days.

Morning light spills on juicy bites,
Melons sing, while grapes take flights.
Bananas crack jokes, all in a bunch,
While oranges giggle, enjoying lunch.

Pineapples wear crowns, quite a sight,
Raspberries blush, feel just right.
We dance in circles, fruit hats askew,
In the garden of joy, there's much to do.

A splash of berry juice, oh so bright,
Twirling around, we take to flight.
The anthem of laughter fills the air,
As apples tumble without a care.

Nectarines whisper, "Come, take a chance,"
While lemons squeeze in a zesty dance.
Such fruity days, where humor thrives,
In our little world, joy comes alive.

Sunlit Whispers in the Orchard

Beneath the branches, shadows play,
As whispers linger through the day.
A bunny hops, claiming its throne,
While giggles rise like wind-blown foam.

Bees are buzzing, quite the show,
Trying to steal the fruits we grow.
Picking apples, tossing them high,
A tumble here, a laugh, oh my!

Cherry trees gossip, never quite still,
While we plot tricks, just for the thrill.
A picnic blanket, our little base,
Filled with laughter, joy, and grace.

Golden rays peek through the leaves,
As we tell secrets, no one believes.
In this orchard, so lush and grand,
Sunlit whispers unite our band.

Joyful Slices of Afternoon

With watermelon smiles, we begin to slice,
Each juicy piece, a tiny paradise.
Laughter spills like seeds on the ground,
No worries here, just joy all around.

Chasing butterflies, they dodge our reach,
With rubbery legs, we try to preach.
The silly faces we make for fun,
A race with shadows beneath the sun.

Ice-cold drinks, with straws in tow,
As we toast to the warmth, our giggles grow.
Playing tag in the light's warm embrace,
Every stumble becomes a race.

Time slows down, in this golden glow,
Where every slice leads to another show.
Joyful afternoons, forever we'll keep,
In laughter and love, our hearts take a leap.

Delicate Moments of Pure Bliss

A slip on a peel, we both start to laugh,
Rolling on grass, oh, what a gaffe!
Sunshine above, and trouble below,
We capture each giggle, let good vibes flow.

A splatter of juice, right on my nose,
I point and I laugh, your cheekiness shows!
Silly old puns, our favorite refrain,
In this lovely chaos, there's no room for pain.

We dance like the leaves, rustling around,
In the breeze we twirl, with joy we are crowned.
With every small stumble, every new slip,
We're snorting with laughter, let's take another trip.

In kitchens we cheer, making a mess,
Flour in our hair, oh, what a dress!
While baking our dreams, sometimes they burn,
Yet each mishap's a tale, in humor we turn.

The Essence of Togetherness

Two mismatched socks, a sight to behold,
In the light of the fridge, your stories unfold.
Dancing with treats, your laughter abounds,
Turning a frown into joy that surrounds.

Sharing a drink, the bubbles take flight,
You splash with a wink, oh, what a sight!
Sweet moments brewed with mischief and cheer,
In our funny romps, life's better my dear.

Pudding on spoons, we both start to race,
Who'll get the last drop? It's a funny chase!
With tangled up spoons, and a playful glance,
In messy delight, we both take a chance.

In cozy old chairs, we plot and we scheme,
Together we reign, like a whimsical dream.
Silly old secrets, we whisper them right,
These moments are treasures, they shine ever bright.

Soft Light on Juicy Tang

Morning sun shining, on fruits piled high,
A squirt of fresh juice, oh my, oh my!
Breakfast in colors, like rainbows on plates,
A taste of sweet laughter, life celebrates.

You trip on a grape, and I can't help but cackle,
With laughter like music, we dance in a tackle.
Slipping on smoothness, upside-down giggles,
In our fruit-laden world, we wiggle and wiggles!

The zest of a citrus, so fresh and so bright,
We brighten the kitchen with silly delight.
As we chop up the veggies, and flip-flop around,
Our culinary capers make life so profound.

With forks in a tussle, pie fights ensue,
Dessert on your nose, it's a sticky déjà vu!
In sweetness and savor, laughter reigns supreme,
Like sorbet on a summer's day, it's the sweetest dream.

Vibrancy in Simple Corners

A corner of joy, where laughter resides,
Painted with colors that nobody hides.
A sock puppet show, we put on for fun,
With jokes and with jests, we dance in the sun.

Pillows as castles, we bounce with pure glee,
Imaginary crowns, you're the queen, oh me!
Face painted smiles, our creativity soars,
With tickles and winks, let's open new doors.

In vibrant old corners, the oddest things play,
A moment so silly, it brightens the day.
Between every giggle, a spark of delight,
In spaces so small, together we light.

With echoes of laughter that linger and glow,
These moments we capture, let our hearts flow.
In the back of the house, we craft memories bright,
With every small corner, we chase pure delight.

Chasing Butterflies and Serenity

In the meadow, I prance and leap,
With butterflies swirling, I can't help but peep.
They're teasing my shoes, a whimsical dance,
Each flit and flutter gives my heart a chance.

A chase turns into giggles and spins,
As I trip on my shoelace, oh where do I begin?
The butterflies laugh, oh what a sight,
I roll on the grass, feeling delight.

Who knew serenity could be so absurd?
With petals in my hair, I must look quite stirred.
But in this field, I feel so alive,
Chasing moments where joy can thrive.

So here's to the day, with laughter to spare,
With bright wings above, and chaos in the air.
I'll try and catch them, that's the game,
In this silly pursuit, no two are the same.

Colorful Mementos from the Garden

In the garden, a treasure of hues,
Where daisies and zinnias sing their own blues.
I gather bright petals, a bouquet of cheer,
Each bloom tells a story, oh dear, oh dear!

A bee buzzes by, quite full of ambition,
It lands on my nose, what a funny position!
I swat it away, now it's time to reflect,
What colorful chaos does Mother Nature select?

Roses are red, but so are my cheeks,
When I trip on a trowel, the garden just squeaks.
With muddy hands, and laughter so wide,
These mementos of joy, I can't help but bide.

So let's skip through petals, laugh through the dew,
With memories of flowers, I'll share them with you.
For each plucked petal holds a giggle in store,
In my garden of wonders, there's always much more.

The Garden of Gentle Moments

Amidst daisies dancing, and soft, gentle breeze,
I find silly thoughts that are sure to appease.
The sun winks playfully, shadows hide and seek,
In a world full of whimsy, it's laughter I seek.

A squirrel steals a snack, oh what a thief!
I clap my hands, feeling disbelief.
With each little scamper, he looks quite the star,
In this garden of chuckles, he's gone too far.

Beneath the big oak, I plop down to rest,
But ants start a parade, they're feeling quite blessed.
They march up my leg, oh what a ruckus!
In this gentle garden, it's fun that comes to discuss.

So here I will sit, with laughter in bloom,
Amidst all the giggles, there's never a gloom.
With moments so gentle, I count them like sheep,
In this garden of laughter, my heart takes a leap.

Exploring Sun-Drenched Paths

Through sun-drenched trails where the wildflowers sway,

I stroll through the laughter of a glorious day.
A butterfly flaps, then lands in my hair,
I'm a mobile garden—oh, how do I fare?

With each tiny step, my worries take flight,
As I stumble on stones, then giggle with delight.
The sun shines so bright, I squint like a fool,
But in this wild world, I'm nobody's tool.

A picnic awaits with treats piled high,
But bees think I'm tasty—a real fly-by.
I swat and I scream, it's a real comic chase,
In this sun-drenched playground, I'm losing my grace.

So I'll wander these paths till the daylight is done,
With antics and laughter, the best kind of fun.
For exploring these trails brings joy on repeat,
In the warmth of the sun, with life oh so sweet.

Savoring Fleeting Seconds

A cat in a box, peeking out,
Who knew cardboard could bring such clout?
It leaps like a ninja, with grace unrestrained,
A fleeting moment, wonderfully obtained.

The ice cream cone, a drippy delight,
It slips from my hand, oh what a sight!
A chorus of giggles from kids all around,
As I chase the blob that rolls on the ground.

A splash in the puddle, heart full of cheer,
I dance like a fool, with no one to fear.
Each drop is a laugh, as the rain starts to cease,
In these moments of joy, your spirit finds peace.

So let's toast to the chaos, the laughter, the play,
These silly little instances, come what may.
For in the grand dance of life's funny scenes,
We cherish the seconds stitched into our dreams.

Radiant Hearts in Bloom

In springtime's embrace, balloons take flight,
Bright colors are twirling, a joyous sight.
The neighbor's dog barks, dressed like a clown,
A furry parade, all decked out in brown.

A picnic set out on a blanket so wide,
With ants doing salsa, as my lunch takes a ride.
I sip lemonade while the sun gives a grin,
And find joy in crumbs that the ants will win.

Laughter erupts at the silliest jokes,
While my dad tries to dance like a flock of old folks.
Each twirl and each swirl, like piñatas in bloom,
Radiance shines from the heart, chasing gloom.

So here's to the glee, to wild moments we share,
In gardens of laughter, found everywhere.
For life is a canvas, painted with cheer,
We find blooming joy in the moments so dear.

Delight Found in the Ordinary

A sock on the floor, it has made a new friend,
A dust bunny joins in, oh what a blend!
They laugh and they roll, round and round they spin,
In the ordinary chaos, where fun does begin.

The toaster goes pop, a bagel takes flight,
Toast lands on my lap—it's a tasty delight!
Crunchy and warm, as crumbs jump and scatter,
Who knew breakfast mess could bring so much chatter?

A trip to the store, it turns into fun,
With a shopping cart race, oh look at them run!
With vegetables flying and giggles galore,
Even mundane tasks open up joy's door.

So here's to the whimsy in all that we do,
In simple little moments, like a cartoon zoo.
For life's quiet wonders are treasures unseen,
In the dance of the ordinary, laughter's routine.

Sunlit Samba of Days

A squirrel on the fence, with acorn in tow,
Practicing moves like a star in the show.
It twirls and it pirouettes, cheeky and spry,
Under sunbeams that shimmer like glitter in the sky.

A kite takes flight in a breezy delight,
It dances on currents, soaring so high.
The kid's laughter bubbles, a melody sweet,
As they zip through the park on their little feet.

A random snowball fight, in the heat of the noon,
Ice cream cones melting like a playful cartoon.
The moment's a swirl of vibrant display,
In sunlit samba, we sway and we play.

So here's to the shenanigans each day brings,
To life's little joys that tickle our wings.
In this dance of delight, may you always find bliss,
In sunlit moments that you simply can't miss.

Lush Days

A sunbeam dances on the ground,
While squirrels in blankets leap around.
Laughter spills like juice from a fruit,
Here, every moment is a hoot!

With jelly on toast and wiggles in feet,
Silly jokes float, a laughter-filled treat.
Mismatched socks sway as they prance,
Inviting all for a silly dance!

Butterflies giggle as they flit,
While bees and birds join in the skit.
Hiccups sneak in during a grin,
Making the fun begin again!

When clouds wear hats and rainbows wink,
We share our secrets over a drink.
The world tilts just so in delight,
As fun bursts out, like stars at night.

Light Hearts

With balloons afloat, up in the sky,
We trade goofy looks, oh my, oh my!
Giggles sprinkle like confetti fair,
In this wild, carefree affair.

Dancing on tiptoes, we twirl and spin,
Each silly step lets the fun begin.
Faces painted with bright, silly glee,
Captured forever, just you and me.

Fizzing drinks bubbling with cheer,
Every clink sounds like laughter near.
A spontaneous game of hide and seek,
Where joy is found in every peek!

With hearts as light as feathered dreams,
We laugh until we burst at the seams.
Moments like these, pure, sweet, and free,
An endless parade of hilarity.

Embraces Wrapped in Warmth

In cozy corners, with blankets to share,
We snuggle and giggle without a care.
Hot cocoa spills with a marshmallow splash,
Laughter erupts with every clash.

Sharing stories that tickle our hearts,
Each chuckle a work of comedic arts.
Warm hugs that squeeze like a big, soft pie,
No moment goes missed with a wink in the eye.

The cat joins in with a clumsy leap,
As we stumble and giggle, falling in heaps.
Fuzzy slippers dance on the floor,
With every embrace, we laugh even more!

Wrapped in joy like gifts in a bow,
This warmth is contagious, you know!
Here, where the smiles are never tailored,
Each moment funnier, genuinely flavored.

Nectar on the Tongue

On sunny days with ice creams abound,
Each drip and drop is a sweet silly sound.
Taste buds burst in a flavor parade,
With every lick, a giggle trade.

Slips and slides in strawberry glee,
Scented memories swirl, come dance with me.
The crunch of cones, a delightful bite,
We joke about toppings from morning to night.

Juicy laughter, tangy and bright,
Fruit-filled delights, pure summer's light.
Jokes fly freely like seeds in the breeze,
Bringing about the brightest of teases.

Every bite is a chance to shine,
Swirls of happiness in every line.
Savor the moments, sweet on the tongue,
As laughter blossoms, forever young.

Harmony in the Peach Blossom Breeze

In the orchard where blossoms bloom,
The air is rich, dispelling all gloom.
With petals that dance, a light-hearted song,
Joy spreads as we hum along.

Bouncing beneath trees with gentle sway,
Every blush on the cheeks, a playful display.
Silly shouts echo, painting the air,
Where laughter and springtime have a fair share.

The sun on our backs, a warm, cozy hug,
Tickling winds feel like a playful tug.
We share sweet secrets by the creek,
With nature's laughter, we're far from meek.

Moments like these, wrapped in delight,
We dance with joy, morning till night.
In the peach blossom breeze, our hearts take flight,
Creating memories, oh what a sight!

Sweet Whispers of Summer

In sunlit fields, we chase the bees,
With sticky fingers and wobbly knees.
Laughter erupts with each little tease,
As we munch on fruit in the warm, soft breeze.

The ice cream truck's jingle, a siren's call,
We sprint in delight, no care for the fall.
Melon juice drips, sticky and small,
We're all giggles and grins, oh, how we sprawl!

Bubbles float up, dancing with glee,
Pop! goes one, now there's just three.
Catching them all, what a sight to see,
We're pirates of fun, on a fruit-filled spree!

As twilight descends, we count the stars,
Squeezing out laughter from our chocolate bars.
With friends and good vibes, we heal all our scars,
In sweet summer nights, we'll drive rusty cars.

Orchard Dreams at Dusk

Under the trees, where shadows play,
We sneak bites of apples, just for today.
Squirrels give side-eyes, who dare come their way,
As laughter swirls 'round, like light in the fray.

The trampoline calls, we bounce high and free,
Landing in piles of leaves, oh what glee!
We giggle like kids, just wild as can be,
Here, laughter is ripe, it's a grand jubilee!

Crickets join in, making their song,
As we roast marshmallows, righting the wrong.
Burned toes and sticky hands, we laugh along,
The night wraps us up, like a cozy sarong.

Whispers of secrets flow in the air,
We tell tales of monsters and who dared to scare.
In our orchard dreams, there's magic to share,
No frowns allowed under the dusk's gentle glare.

Golden Hours of Laughter

With a picnic spread out, oh what a sight,
We toss the food, in our playful fight.
Flying sandwiches, what a blissful delight,
Our giggles echo through the warm, sunny light.

Sunflowers dance, swaying in sync,
We craft silly hats, with just a wink.
Dodging the bees, and drinks that stink,
In this golden hour, our spirits don't shrink.

Chasing rainbows that lead to nowhere,
Daring each other, few thoughts, just flair.
We stumble and laugh, 'cause life's just unfair,
Each moment is treasure, nothing can compare!

As the sun sets low, we gather our gear,
Telling wild tales, friend, far or near.
The warmth of our hearts, nothing can sear,
Golden hours of laughter, forever we cheer!

Blossoms in the Breeze

Petals drift down, like confetti in spring,
We dance in the gardens, while the bees sing.
With icing on cupcakes, we try to take wing,
In this sweet world, we're all just a thing.

Tickling each other as shadows creep near,
With laughter undying, and full of good cheer.
Silly faces made, we have nothing to fear,
Blossoms all around us, drawing us near.

Giggling frogs leap, causing much fuss,
As we splash in puddles without a discuss.
Fingers sticky with honey, oh what a plus,
In these giggly moments, life's a good bus!

With whispered secrets beneath leafy boughs,
We cherish these days, the fun in the now.
Time stands still here, let's take our vows,
To savor these moments, with goofy bows!

Harvesting Happiness from the Branches

In a garden where laughter grows,
We pick the best fruits to impose.
With giggles ripe, we fill our bags,
Jokes falling like leaves, no time for drags.

A squirrel steals a peach with pride,
I shout, 'Hey buddy, what's your side?'
He drops it fast, then runs away,
'That's not yours!' I yell, in playful sway.

The sunbeams dance on our sunny face,
Chasing each other in a lighthearted race.
We trip on roots but laugh it loud,
Nature's a playground, we're so proud!

With each sweet bite, a smile we gain,
Happiness flows, like summer rain.
In every cherish, a tale we weave,
Through branches swaying, we truly believe.

Sun-Drenched Revelations

Under the sun, we wear our hats,
Sharing puns like friendly chats.
A peach rolls by, makes quite a scene,
Wobbling off, it's the star of our dream.

We lounge on the grass, snacks in a pile,
A picnic spread with enough to beguile.
Each bite's a burst, sticky and fun,
Counting the laughs like we count the sun.

The bees are buzzing, but we don't mind,
They join the party, the friendliest kind.
We joke that they're here for the show,
Dancing around us, putting on a glow.

In a moment so silly, we catch our breath,
Life's light-heartedness, a gift 'til death.
With every chuckle, the world feels bright,
Sun-drenched revelry, oh, what a sight!

Embracing the Juicy Present

With juice on our hands and laughter near,
We munch on fruits, each bite a cheer.
A squirrel pokes fun, with a twitch of his tail,
We laugh at the sight, it never gets stale.

Fruits fall down, and we play catch,
Under the tree with a playful match.
With each round, a giggle, a slip,
Nature's delight in every trip.

The sun tickles our toes, what a tease,
Chasing shadows, we do as we please.
Time's not the boss when fun's in the air,
Every moment's juicy, nothing compares!

Let's embrace today with a quirky twist,
With every smile, joy can't be missed.
In this fruit-filled chaos, life's not a test,
We dance through the day, and oh, it's the best!

Heartfelt Moments in the Trees

Up in the branches, we swing with glee,
A world of delight, just you and me.
With every rustle, secrets take flight,
In a heart-shaped nook, our spirits ignite.

We throw down jokes like ripened fruit,
With punchlines so sharp, they leave a hoot.
The tree becomes home to our laughter's song,
As we soar through the air, nothing feels wrong.

We scribble our dreams on bark with a grin,
Celebrating each twist, letting joy sink in.
The leaves applaud with a gentle sway,
While we etch sweet moments to cherish each day.

In this playful space, where friendship blooms,
With hearty chuckles, we chase away glooms.
Embracing the antics, fall's here to tease,
Heartfelt moments linger, swaying in the trees.

Ephemeral Joy with Sweet Effect

A banana slipped, oh what a sight,
Made me chuckle with pure delight.
Faces turned red, laughter flowed free,
In moments so silly, we all just agree.

Chasing the ice cream truck down the lane,
Screams and giggles, pleasure not pain.
Falling on grass, like out of a dream,
Joy in the chaos, a whimsical theme.

Unexpected rain, it poured like confetti,
Umbrellas flipped over, the scene was quite petty.
Dancing in puddles, splashing around,
In such messy moments, pure joy is found.

With friends gathered 'round, we feast and we share,
The pizza's half gone, but no one would care.
In laughter we bloom, like flowers in spring,
These fleeting soft seconds, oh what joy they bring.

Friendly Chats and Afternoon Bliss

In the park we laze, sipping our drinks,
Swapping wild stories, and sharing our links.
Puppies roam by, stealing our snacks,
The laughter is loud, as humor attacks.

A kite took off, dancing so high,
We cheered and we joked, reaching for the sky.
Then a gust came through, oh what a surprise,
We tangled our strings, laughing at our ties.

Gossiping while birds do their thing,
A warm breeze hits, and we start to sing.
With each silly tale, our bond grows tight,
In moments like these, life feels just right.

A round of ice cream, so sweet, what a treat,
Sticky hands and faces, the ultimate feat.
We relish these chats, sun shining so bright,
In joy-filled hours, our spirits take flight.

Warm Vistas of Laughter

Up on the hill, we see the whole town,
Goofy faces, no reason to frown.
A squirrel stole my sandwich, oh what a pick,
It dashed off so fast, it was quite the trick.

Hats flew away with a gust of the breeze,
We chased them in circles, like kids if you please.
Each stumble and trip turned into new jokes,
As laughter echoed from all of us folks.

With each silly dance in this playful retreat,
We twirled under sunlight, our hearts skipping beats.
Catching fireflies, until dark hugs the light,
These warm vistas of laughter glow through the night.

Picnics turned wild, with ants acting fast,
Our snacks disappeared, it was quite the blast.
On days filled with smiles, we bask sunny-hued,
In warm vistas of laughter, our spirits renewed.

Respite in Nature's Serenity

Whispers of leaves in the balmy breeze,
With a funny friend, tensions all cease.
A slip on a log sends us into giggles,
Nature's own stage, as our joy wiggles.

Cloud shapes like dragons drift overhead,
We talk about dreams while lying down spread.
Then a frog leapt, causing fitful shrieks,
In the heart of the wild, laughter peaks.

An echoing shout, "Where's my shoe gone?"
A raccoon grinned, but it was long gone.
As branches sway lightly, we chase after cheer,
In nature's embrace, smiles draw near.

Sipping on juice, with grass stains on knees,
We soak every moment; oh, can we freeze?
In the beauty around, our worries burn low,
Respite in nature, that's where we glow.

Radiant Memories of Youth

Kites flying high in the clear, blue sky,
We'd giggle and tumble, oh me, oh my!
Sticky fingers smudged with jam and cream,
Chasing the ice cream truck, what a dream!

Sneaking cookies from the jar, oh so sly,
Climbing trees, daring the clouds to fly.
Whispers of secrets shared under the stars,
Creating wild stories of martians from Mars.

Days spent in puddles, splashing with flair,
Wearing mismatched socks, not a worry or care.
Each silly dance move, a memory bright,
Wrapped in laughter, the world felt just right.

So here's to those days, each chuckle resounds,
With friends by our sides, adventure abounds!
A toast to the joys that we boldly embraced,
Forever in heart, never to be replaced.

The Dance of Sunlight and Shadows

Dancing in sunlight, shadows at play,
Twisting and twirling, we'd laugh the whole way.
With each little skip, we'd make a great sound,
As the light played tricks, all joy was unbound.

Sidewalk chalk sidewalks, our canvas so bright,
Drawing silly monsters that danced in delight.
Each hopscotch square marked with giggles and dreams,
While sunlight would wink, or so it seems.

Summer days fleeting, like ice cream that melts,
Chasing the breeze, oh, the joy that it felt!
We'd spin to the rhythm of nature's sweet call,
In the blink of an eye, we'd tumble and fall.

So here's to the moments that spark the pure glee,
In the dance of the shadows, we danced wild and free!
May laughter ring on like a favorite song,
In the sunlight's embrace, where we all belong.

Orchard Adventures in Full Bloom

Under the branches, ripe fruits would beckon,
Adventures a-plenty, our giggles a weapon.
Climbing up trees, each branch an escape,
In a world made of laughter, all shapes, no tape!

Chasing the bees, avoiding their buzz,
Exploring the orchard, just because!
With baskets in hand, we'd gather our scores,
Tasting the sweetness from Mother Nature's stores.

Wobbling on stools for the best pickings,
Nature's buffet set for our silly lickings.
Lemonade spills and that sticky-sweet tone,
With laughter like leaves, how our hearts have grown!

Here's to the moments beneath boughs so grand,
Our childhoods woven like our fingers hand in hand.
In every orchard sprout, a giggle remains,
A treasure of joy, forever it gains.

Serendipity in Every Bite

Bites of delight in the sweetest of treats,
From chocolate to cherries, we'd savor our feats.
Each morsel a giggle, each crumb a new song,
In kitchens and corners, where laughter belongs.

Slipping on sprinkles, making a mess,
Cupcake explosions, oh what a success!
Flour clouds swirling, the chaos divine,
Our friends laughed so hard, they couldn't decline.

With frosting on noses, smiles ear to ear,
Nothing could stop us, we had not a fear.
The joy of our snacks, the fun that we shared,
Each bite held a story, and we were well prepared.

A toast to the flavors that spark silly cheer,
In the warmth of the kitchen, with laughter so near.
May we always find giggles in every dessert,
For life is a feast, oh, how blessed we are hurt!

www.ingramcontent.com/pod-product-compliance
Lightning Source LLC
Chambersburg PA
CBHW060114230426
43661CB00003B/180